A *fashionable* HISTORY of HATS & HAIRSTYLES

A FASHIONABLE HISTORY OF HATS &
HAIRSTYLES
was produced by

David West 🕴️ Children's Books
7 Princeton Court
55 Felsham Road
London SW15 1AZ

Author: Helen Reynolds
Editor: Clare Hibbert
Picture Research: Carlotta Cooper
Designer: Julie Joubinaux

First published in Great Britain in 2003 by
Heinemann Library, Halley Court, Jordan Hill,
Oxford OX2 8EJ, a division of
Harcourt Education Ltd.

OXFORD MELBOURNE AUCKLAND
JOHANNESBURG BLANTYRE GABORONE
IBADAN PORTSMOUTH (NH) USA CHICAGO

07 06 05 04 03
10 9 8 7 6 5 4 3 2 1

ISBN 0 431 18332 5 (HB)
ISBN 0 431 18340 6 (PB)

British Library Cataloguing in Publication Data

Reynolds, Helen
A fashionable history of hats and hairstyles
1. Hats - History - Juvenile literature 2. Hairstyles
- History - Juvenile literature 3. Fashion - History
- Juvenile literature
I. Title II. Hats and hairstyles
391.4'3

Printed and bound in China

PHOTO CREDITS :
Abbreviations: t-top, m-middle, b-bottom, r-right,
l-left, c-centre.

Front cover m, 3 & 10-11 – Mary Evans Picture
Library; br & 27br – Rex Features Ltd.
Pages 4tr, 5tr, 6bl, 7l, 10tr, 11tr, 12bl, 13tr & br,
14tl & br, 16tl, 16-17, 17m, 20 all, 22l & tr, 23l &
r, 24l, 25tl, 26tr & bl, 28tl, 28-29b – Mary Evans
Picture Library. 4br, 6br, 10l & br, 12br, 13bl,
14bl, 15l & bm, 16bm, 18bl, 18-19t, 22br, 26r –
Dover Books. 5tl & b, 6tr, 12tr, 16bl, 18tl, 21tr &
bl, 25bl, 27tl – The Culture Archive. 7tr –
ISG113867 A Young Lady of Fashion (oil on
panel) by Paolo Uccello (1397-1475), Isabella
Stewart Gardner Museum, Boston, Massachusetts,
USA/Bridgeman Art Library. 7br, 28-29t, 29mr –
Hulton Archive. 8bl & tr, 8-9b, 9 both, 11bl & br,
15tr & mr, 17tl & tr, 19br, 21m & br, 23tm, 24br,
25m & br, 26-27, 29bm – Rex Features Ltd. 17mr
– Karen Augusta, www.antique-fashion.com. 19tl,
tm & tr – Corbis Images. 28bl – Katz/FSP.

Every effort has been made to contact copyright
holders of any material reproduced in this book.
Any omissions will be rectified in subsequent
printings if notice is given to the publishers.

*An explanation of difficult words can be
found in the glossary on page 31.*

A *fashionable* HISTORY of HATS & HAIRSTYLES

Heinemann
LIBRARY

Contents

Barber's pole

A striped pole is the traditional sign for a barber's shop.

Medieval hats

In the Middle Ages, rich European women wore fantastically tall hats, draped with fluttering veils.

Hats & hairstyles

MORE THAN ANY OTHER BODY ADORNMENT, hats and hairstyles reflect not only the fashions of the day, but also a person's social status – and even religious beliefs. Head coverings offer protection and warmth, but also mark a person's position in society. Until recently, ornate hairstyles and hats were only for the rich. Workers wore practical hats and dressed their hair simply.

Today, crowns, judges' wigs and military berets still mark rank. However, hats and hairstyles are usually a fashion statement rather than a sign of status.

VICTORIAN ADVERTISEMENT
In the 1800s it was not fashionable to change hair colour. However, many people resorted to dyes to cover greying hair.

A TRIP TO THE SALON
Bouffant hairdos of the 1950s had to be set under dryers at the hairdresser's.

Hats
The bicorn (c.1800) was a crescent-shaped man's hat. This picture also shows early top hats.

Hair history

SINCE EARLY TIMES HAIRSTYLES HAVE SHOWN BEAUTY – AND POWER. *The Old Testament warrior Samson (or Shimshon, in the Jewish faith) made a holy vow not to cut his hair, for example. He lost his strength when his head was shorn. Haircuts and styles could also be a sign of status. Wealthy ancient Assyrians arranged their hair in fancy curls, while Egyptians shaved their heads and wore glossy wigs.*

The long hair story

In ancient Greece and Rome, men kept their hair short, but the only women with short hair were slaves. Although exact fashions changed, noblewomen wore their long hair braided and knotted. They even used hair dye. In Europe, there was a new craze for classical styles in the late 1700s, following the discovery of a ruined Roman town at Pompeii, Italy.

EGYPTIAN SIDELOCK

Egyptian nobles had shaved heads, but during their youth they kept one sidelock of long hair.

CURLY STYLES

In the 1830s, women wore their hair in neat buns and chignons, with tight ringlets twirling down at the sides. Curls were fashionable for men, too.

ROMAN LADY

In ancient Rome, slaves styled their mistresses' hair. They used heated irons to create masses of tiny curls. These were held back from the face by hairpins of precious ivory or bone.

TRADITIONAL JAPANESE COIFFURE

These Japanese Court fashions of 1890 had changed little since the 1100s, when they were copied from the Chinese. Long hair was lacquered and then secured with elegant combs and hairsticks.

15TH-CENTURY SKINHEAD

Renaissance ladies plucked their hairline to achieve a high forehead. Hair, when not covered, was usually tied or plaited around the head.

Short cuts

Women's styles stayed long until around World War I (1914–18). Then, the famous ballroom dancer Irene Castle (1893–1969) cut her hair in a boyish bob. By the 1920s, many young women were cutting their hair. The bob gave way to the shingle, which was snipped closer to the head. An even shorter version was the Eton crop, named after schoolboys' short haircuts.

BIRTH OF THE BOB

Movie star Louise Brooks (1906–85) was one of the first famous women to go short. She sported a straight, sleek bob.

Alternative styles

THE BOB WAS CONSIDERED SHOCKING WHEN IT FIRST APPEARED, *but to some of the young women who wore it, the style was more than just a fashion. It was a symbol of their equality with men, after winning the right to vote. The bob reappeared during another period of freedom and change – the 1960s. Vidal Sassoon (b.1929) brought out his five-point bob in 1964. As the decade progressed, young people began to see that how they dressed, and how they wore their hair, could express their individuality, identity, and the way they felt about society.*

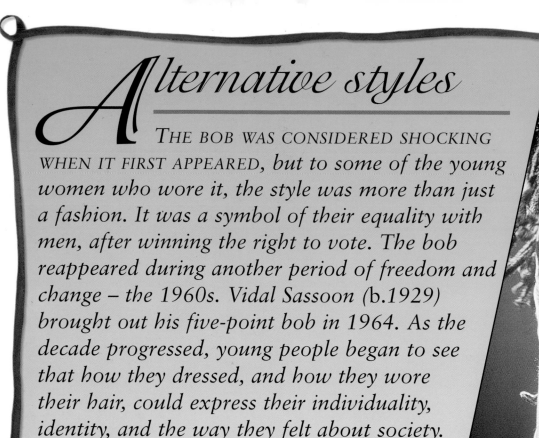

LENNY KRAVITZ
Kravitz (b.1964) wears dreadlocks – long, twisty locks of matted hair.

MADE TO MELT
Punks liked to shock by styling their hair into an outlandish, spiky crest called a mohican. The punk on the left has created a sweet version – out of icecream cones!

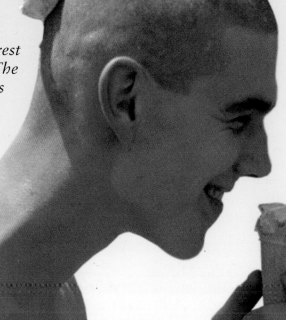

BATMAN BONCE!
Shaved heads look funky and can be fun, too. Motifs are made by masking an area of hair before clipping.

Express yourself!

From the late 1960s, black people began to celebrate their identity through their hair. They stopped straightening their hair so it conformed to neat, 'white' styles. Followers of the black religion Rastafarianism grew their hair into long, matted dreadlocks. Other styles adopted to express black pride include the afro, and African-style braiding.

Young people often adopt a hairstyle to show they are part of a group. Close-cropped hair may be mainstream today, but the style was first worn by skinheads to express no-nonsense aggression. Punks, too, used shocking styles to show they were outside 'normal' society, and that they rejected its values.

Ace afro

American actress Marsha Hunt (b.1946) grew her hair into a distinctive afro. People of African origin, like Hunt, often have naturally curly, bushy hair, and the afro emphasizes these qualities with pride. But although the hair looks natural, it actually takes a lot of styling. Strands of hair have to be teased out with a special afro comb.

A little bit of this & that: The mullet

Long hair is popular with men who do not need to look clean-cut for the office. The 1980s was the age of the mullet – a compromise style that was long at the back, but short on the top and at the sides.

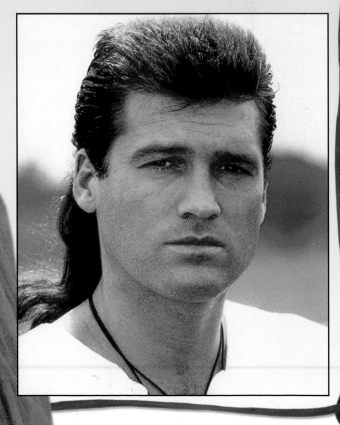

Wigs

ANCIENT EGYPTIANS WORE WIGS *if they were part of the nobility, over closely-shaved heads. Men's wigs were short and blunt-fringed, while women wore longer wigs of plaited, twisted hair.*

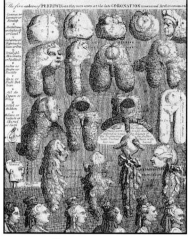

Costly choices

These wigs of the 1700s were expensive. Only the wealthy had several.

Wigging out

Wigs were popular with wealthy people in 17th-century Europe, too. People did not have hot water on tap and dirty, greasy hair was a problem. Many men chose to shave their head and wear a wig instead. Wigs were usually made of human, yak or horsehair and came in a staggering range of styles – long or short, straight, curled or frizzed. By the 1730s, some wigs were dusted with white wig powder, which could be scented with orange blossom or lavender. The white, full-bottom wig worn by English judges dates from this period.

Nile style

Thick, glossy black wigs were worn in ancient Egypt by the nobility. Some were ornately plaited with gold and silver threads.

Wig-making

Some 18th-century wigs were in natural colours, but the most fashionable were white. Many were tied at the back with a black ribbon.

The decline of the wig?

By 1800, wigs were no longer in fashion although they were still worn by people who lost their hair naturally or through illness. The costliest wigs were made of human hair, and selling one's locks could raise a lot of money. Today, wigs are far less common. It is more acceptable to be bald than to wear a wig – unless it is a dayglo party wig, of course!

Wig cartoon of 1780

Wigs grew to enormous heights – and harboured all sorts of vermin!

Puff of powder

18th-century barbers were kept busy cleaning, curling and powdering their clients' wigs. They also sold long wig scratchers made of ivory or bone. Men used these to scratch at the nits – or mice – that often burrowed into their wigs!

Top toupee

Actor Burt Reynolds (b.1936) is famous for his toupees (hairpieces). He wears them to disguise his receding hairline.

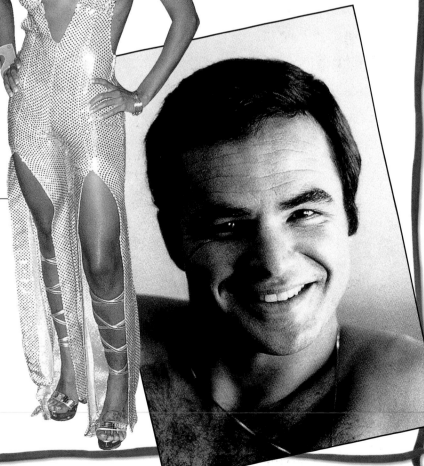

Party wigs

Wigs are far more convenient than coloured dyes for women who want a fun, party look. Pop star Lisa Lopes (1971–2002) wore a bright green wig when she hosted the Music of Black Origin Awards in London, 2000.

All sorts of adornments

ELABORATE HAIR DECORATIONS HAVE BEEN POPULAR *since ancient times. The Egyptians wove jewels into their wigs, while in ancient Greece and Rome women wore gold, silver and jewelled hair-bands. Not all adornments were purely decorative. Julius Caesar (100–44 BCE) is said to have adopted the laurel wreath to cover his bald patch!*

Meltingly sweet scents

The Egyptians sometimes placed cones of scented wax on top of their wigs. As the wax melted it dripped over the wig, making it look glossy – and smell gorgeous!

Braids & nets

In 12th-century Europe, women either covered their hair or wore it in long plaits, criss-crossed with braid. From the 1200s, women's hair was increasingly covered with a veil, mantle (hooded cloak) or headdress. From the 1400s, in southern Europe, hair was worn loose with a simple circlet, or braided and pinned into fillets.

Geisha girl

Japanese geishas were known for their great beauty. They wore costly ornamental combs and hairpins called kanzashi.

Circlets & fillets

Early Renaissance women (c.1500s) brushed back their hair and pinned it. They wore circlets, fillets and hairnets decorated with gold, silver and jewels.

Curls, feathers & combs

From the late 1700s, Greek-inspired ornaments were popular, worn with classical curls. Strips of cloth called bandeaux were wrapped around the head and sometimes finished with outsize feathers. By 1820, fashionable hair was often worn in a plaited knot, held in place with decorative hairpins and combs.

Tall plumes

In the 1790s, many women increased their height by wearing tall feathers in their hair – but some took the fashion too far!

Blooming lovely!

In the early 1900s, women often used fresh or silk flowers as hair decorations. Maids were specially trained to pile the hair high and weave in lots of pretty blooms.

Evening bandeau

The bandeau made a comeback in the 1920s as a way to jazz up short styles. The jewellery company Cartier (founded 1847) even designed priceless bands of diamonds.

Religion & ceremony

ALMOST EVERY RELIGION HAS SPECIAL FORMS OF HEADWEAR – *worn all the time as a constant reminder of faith, or only for religious ceremonies. Native American Indians, for example, traditionally wear elaborate, feathered headdresses for their rituals. State occasions, too, require special headwear.*

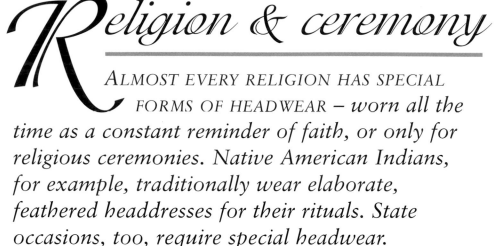

EGYPTIAN KING IN BATTLE

From 3100 BCE, pharaohs wore tall crowns to mark kingship. The battle crown, or khepresh, was usually made of leather. It was decorated with gold or bronze discs.

Crowns for kings & queens

Rulers in ancient Egypt and Assyria were probably the first to wear crowns. The Egyptian pharaoh wore a double crown to show that two lands – Upper and Lower Egypt – were united under his control. Since then, crowns have often been a symbol of supreme authority, worn by emperors, tsars and kings. The start of a ruler's reign is usually marked by a coronation, or crowning ceremony.

KINGLY CROWN

Medieval rulers wore gem-studded crowns of iron, bronze, silver or gold.

BISHOPS' MITRES

Bishops and archbishops wear tall, decorative hats called mitres. They are shaped to point up to heaven.

Religious headdresses & hair

Hats and hair can be a sign of faith. Many Muslim women wear a headscarf called a hejab, while the men wear a prayer cap called a kufi. Orthodox Jews cover their heads, too. The men wear black hats, but many women find it easier to cover their hair by wearing a wig. Buddhist and Christian monks may shave their heads as a sign of humility before God.

The Sikh turban

To show they are part of one family, all Sikhs wear the Five Ks. These are the kirpan (dagger), kangha (comb), kara (bangle), kaccha (pants) and kesh (uncut hair). The turban is not one of the Five Ks, but Sikh males wear it to keep the kesh tidy.

Monk's tonsure

Monks shave their heads in a style called a tonsure. The circle of hair represents Christ's crown of thorns.

The yarmulke

All Jewish men wear a skullcap called a kippah or yarmulke when they pray.

Nun's headdress

Some nuns' habits include a dark veil which is held in place with a white band called a coif. A white wimple covers the throat.

Weather protection

LONG BEFORE THEY WERE FASHION ITEMS, HATS WERE WORN *for warmth or as defence against the elements. The ancient Greeks, for example, wore straw sunhats called petasos.*

Fur & feathers

19th century American fur trappers wore bear- or raccoon-skin hats to keep them warm in the mountains.

Rain *or shine*

Fur, felt, wool and, recently, synthetic fleece provide the best insulation against the cold. The first waterproof hats appeared in the 1800s. The sou-wester was a sailor's hat. It was made of rubber or oilskin, and specially shaped so any rainwater would run off the wide brim at the back.

Sunhats were very popular in the 1800s, as people prized their pale complexions. Ladies' bonnets had wide brims to protect them from the sun. Men wore straw boaters. A hat cover, called a havelock, was worn by men in hot climates. It had a back flap to protect the neck.

Storm ahead!

Sou-westers were traditionally worn at sea. They are named after rain-bearing south-westerly winds.

Motoring hats

Ladies travelling in the first, open-top cars wore special hats to protect their hair from the wind – and dust.

Straw boaters, 1930s

Boaters are stiff straw sunhats trimmed with a heavy, corded ribbon, known as petersham ribbon. This advert is from the 1930s although they were popular with men in the late 19th century.

Super shady

Popular in Spain and Mexico, the sombrero has an enormous brim that gives all-round shade from the sun.

Field fashion

In Southeast Asia, workers are busy in the rice fields all day. They wear wide, veiled sunhats.

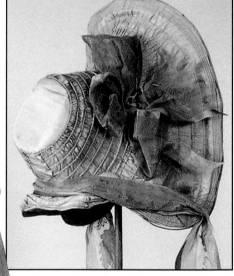

Cleverly collapsible

Hats can be bulky to store, but some are designed to go flat. 19th-century ladies often wore a calash – a silk hood on a folding, whalebone frame. The panama is a man's sunhat from Ecuador. Even when rolled flat to fit in a suitcase, it will spring back to its original shape.

Sun bonnets

Poke-bonnets were usually made of straw. The large poke, or front brim, protected the wearer's nose from sunburn.

Return of the hat!

When tans became fashionable in the 1920s, sunhats went out of fashion. However, recent worries about links between suntans and skin cancer have led to increased sunhat sales once more.

Sporting style

The American baseball cap is now the most widely-worn sunhat. It was popularized in the 1920s and 1930s, by the baseball star Babe Ruth (1895–1948).

Helmets for heroes

HELMETS ORIGINALLY DEVELOPED AS BATTLE DRESS and they safeguard the head from hard knocks. The style of a battle helmet was always very important too, because it identified which side a soldier was on.

From horse skulls to haute couture

Ancient Ethiopian warriors are said to have worn horse skulls, complete with flowing manes, as helmets! However, most early helmets were made of leather or metal. Medieval knights wore steel helmets as part of their armour. Plate armour was strongest, but also extremely heavy. Chainmail was lighter and could withstand sword thrusts, but not showers of arrows. In the late 1960s, medieval chainmail made a high-fashion comeback when Spanish designer Paco Rabanne (*b*.1934) brought out metal-linked mini-dresses with matching helmets.

Hoplite's helmet

Greek hoplites (foot soldiers) had helmets of hammered bronze, with horsehair crests. Their helmets were the first to have a nose shield.

Victorious gladiator

Gladiators fought to the death as entertainment for the ancient Romans. Some were equipped with limited armour, such as a helmet, sword and shield.

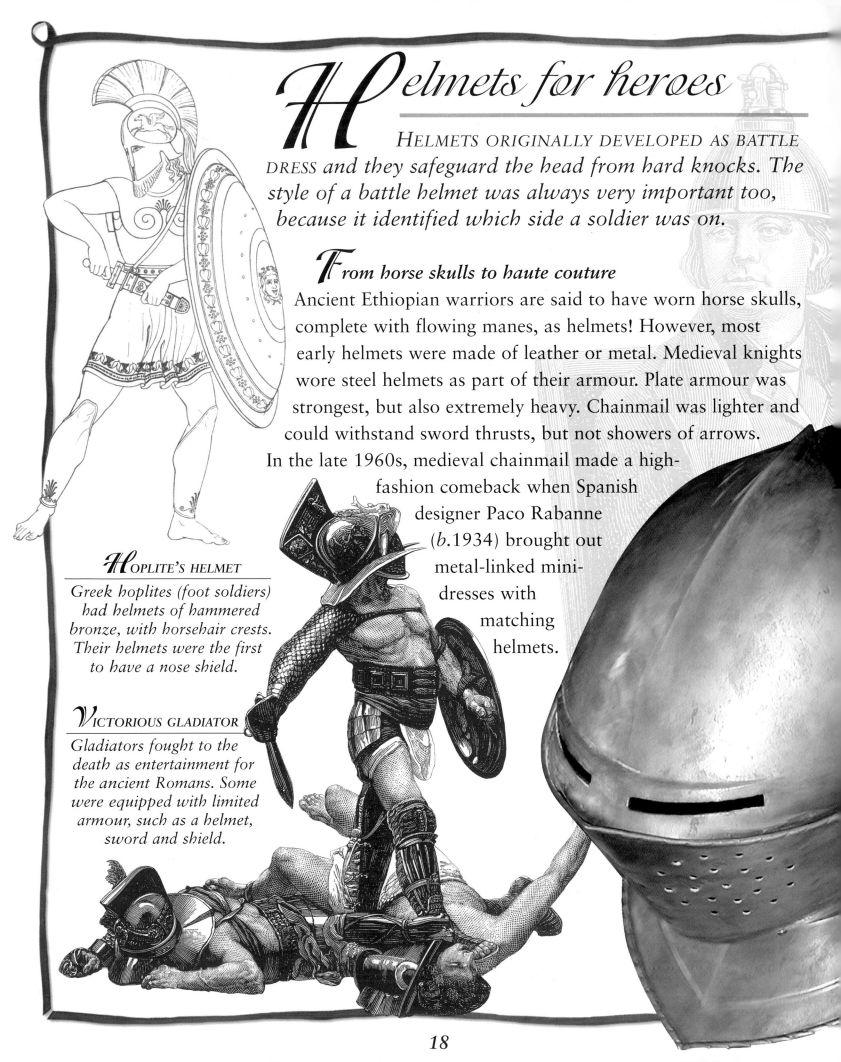

Hard Hats

Helmets protect construction workers' heads from falling masonry or machinery.

Helmets for Today's Armed Forces

A modern fighter pilot's helmet has a glare-free visor and easily hooks up to an oxygen supply. For soldiers on the ground (inset), helmets protect against bombs and bullets. Camouflage is all-important.

Hard-wearing, hard-working

Today, soldiers wear helmets made of super-strong synthetic materials such as Kevlar. These offer more protection than ever before and are lightweight and easy to wear.

Protective helmets are also worn by police, firefighters and on building sites. Motorcylists put on crash-helmets to protect their heads, and jockeys wear reinforced riding hats in case they are thrown from their horse. Other sports where helmets are worn include cycling, skateboarding, ice hockey, baseball and American football.

American Footballer

A cage at the front of this footballer's helmet shields his easily-broken nose and teeth.

Medieval Plate Helmet

Knights' helmets were usually made from steel. The hinged visor had eye slits and breathing holes. Helmets were sometimes engraved with family crests.

Headscarves & turbans

THE CLASSIC HEADWRAP IS THE EASTERN TURBAN, but Westerners were wearing similar head coverings over a thousand years ago. For women, there was the coverchief, a square or semi-circle of linen that wrapped around the head and neck leaving the face exposed. For men, there was the bourrelet, a roll of fabric worn under a hood called a chaperon.

High hood, 1300s

Medieval noblemen wore a turban-style hood called a chaperon. The headwrap underneath was called a bourrelet.

Gifts from the East

Eastern-style turbans became fashionable in the West during the 1700s as it became usual for rich, young Europeans to go off on grand tours. Some men adopted the exotic headdresses of the places they visited, wearing the turban when relaxing at home. By the end of the century, turbans were part of women's evening dress. They were often lavishly decorated with ostrich plumes and sparkling jewels. French designer Paul Poiret (1879–1944) revived the look in 1909 when he created a collection of orientally-inspired costumes.

Ladies' headwraps

Medieval women wore a veil over their coverchief, or headwrap (c.1200s). Together called a wimple, it was secured with a circlet.

Cashmere and muslin turbans

Romantic poets such as Lord Byron (1788–1824) wrote of exotic places and often wore costumes to match. Women adopted turbans in fine fabrics too, as illustrated in 1833 (left) – perfect foils for the high, wide hairstyles.

Silken squares

The 20th century saw the rise of the headscarf. A practical item for women at work, the scarf became a fashion item during the 1950s. The Parisian saddle company Hermès (founded in 1837) produced expensive silk squares with horsey motifs that were widely copied. Hermès scarves remain popular at high-society sporting events – one of the company's most famous customers is Queen Elizabeth (*b.*1926).

War worker

This headscarf of 1943 was typical of women on war work. It kept hair clean and safe from factory machinery.

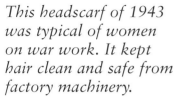

Chic sheiks on screen

Many Hollywood movies from the 1920s featured Middle Eastern themes. Starlets and other fashionable women started wearing turbans and headscarves as a result.

Jaunty!

In the 1950s, patterned silk, satin or nylon headscarves were very fashionable as casual wear. The square scarf folded in half to make a triangular shape and knotted under the chin.

Desert wrap

Kaffiyehs are headdresses worn by Arab men. They give protection against sandstorms, and the strong desert sun.

Tall hats

IN MEDIEVAL EUROPE, HATS BECAME *very elaborate and ostentatious. Smooth, high foreheads were considered very elegant, so fashionable women scraped back their hair and wore tall hats for extra emphasis.*

Medieval hats, 11th & 13th centuries

In the Middle Ages, noblewomen wore horned headdresses (with two turrets) and hennins (with a single steeple). Both were around a metre tall and strung with long, gauzy veils.

Horns & hennins

Twin turrets were added to the square wimple to create a horned headdress – similar in style to the hats worn today by Dutch women as part of their national dress. In Europe, from around 1450, a single-turret steeple-hat called a hennin was worn.

Crowning glories

In the early 1600s a high-crowned, small-brimmed hat called the capotain was worn by both sexes. Even after it went out of fashion, the hat remained popular with the Puritans (Protestants who wanted Church reforms).

Puritan in sugarloaf hat

Puritans dressed plainly. They named their high-crowned capotains 'sugarloaf hats', because they were cone-shaped, just like tall mounds of refined sugar.

High hat

Like the Victorian British bobby's headwear, this American policeman's hat of the early 20th century added height and deflected blows.

Top hat

The shiny silk top hat, pictured here in the 1800s, was first worn with day or evening wear.

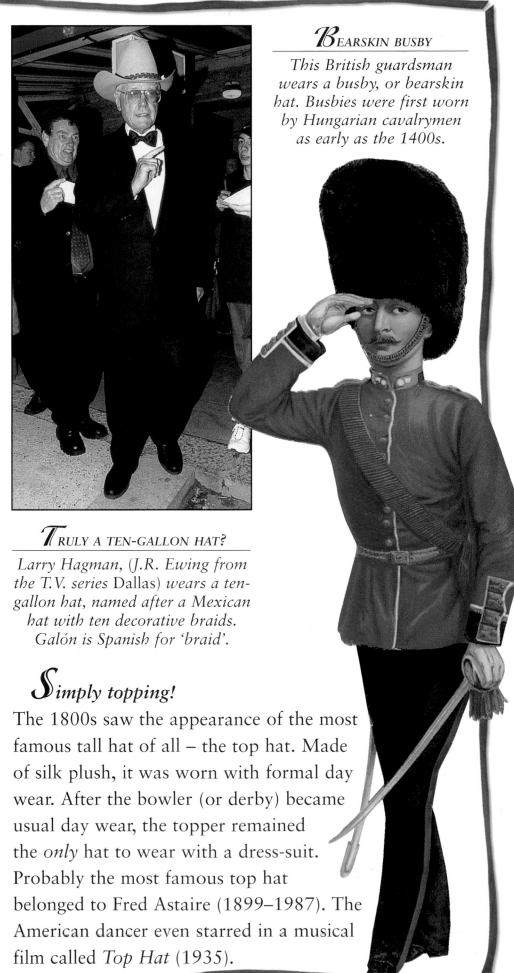

Bearskin busby

This British guardsman wears a busby, or bearskin hat. Busbies were first worn by Hungarian cavalrymen as early as the 1400s.

Truly a ten-gallon hat?

Larry Hagman, (J.R. Ewing from the T.V. series *Dallas*) *wears a ten-gallon hat, named after a Mexican hat with ten decorative braids. Galón is Spanish for 'braid'.*

Simply topping!

The 1800s saw the appearance of the most famous tall hat of all – the top hat. Made of silk plush, it was worn with formal day wear. After the bowler (or derby) became usual day wear, the topper remained the *only* hat to wear with a dress-suit. Probably the most famous top hat belonged to Fred Astaire (1899–1987). The American dancer even starred in a musical film called *Top Hat* (1935).

Flat hats

IN THE 1500s, MEN AND WOMEN BEGAN TO WEAR FLATTER HATS. One close-fitting hat was the toque, which was usually brimless. Velvet berets, perhaps trimmed with fur, were also popular, worn sloping to the side. In the 1600s, hats stayed relatively flat, but developed a broad brim that could be decorated with an ostrich feather.

Simple... & not-so-simple

As the hats worn by the nobility became wider and more ostentatious, Puritan women opted for plain, white linen caps. Similar caps were worn at home by ladies and gentlemen of the nobility, to keep off draughts. By the 1700s, these had developed into fancy boudoir or morning caps. They were worn by leisured women to cover rumpled or undressed hair.

FASHIONABLE FELT

In the 16th century, stiff, felt caps were worn indoors and out. The brim often turned up at the front, and was held in place by a single jewel. Rich red was a highly fashionable hat colour.

PILL-BOX

U.S. First Lady Jackie Kennedy (1929–94) wore felt pill-boxes, designed by Roy Halston (1932–90), in the sixties. They had first appeared in the 1930s. This model's 'tilted' example is from 1953.

Flat-caps for all

Flat, woollen caps are easy to produce and cheap. From the 1600s, they were worn for warmth by labourers and apprentices. In the late 1800s, these developed a peak at the front. Flat-caps were no longer worn only by the working classes. The upper classes wore tweed ones for sports, such as shooting or golf, while the middle classes wore them for cycling and hiking. However, unlike working men, gentlemen never wore a flat-cap in town. During the 1960s, fashionable young women wore flat-caps made of PVC or leather, after André Courrèges (b.1923) teamed them with his catsuits and miniskirts.

CUTE, CROCHETED CAPS

Knitting and crocheting were popular pastimes in the 1940s. Colourful caps could be crocheted using just a few leftover scraps of wool.

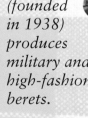

THE BERET

French workers wear a flat-cap called a beret. It is also part of many soldiers' uniforms. Kangol (founded in 1938) produces military and high-fashion berets.

TARTAN TAM-O'-SHANTERS

Exaggerated takes on the Scottish tam-o'-shanter are popular with football fans.

THE WORKING MAN'S FLAT-CAP

In this 19th-century photograph, only the manual workers wear flat-caps. The cap became a symbol of the working class.

Outrageous hats

For the last 50 years, it has no longer been necessary for men and women to be hatted when they go out. Today, more than ever before, hats are worn only for special occasions, and designer hats can cost more than the rest of the outfit put together! Modern milliners delight in designing eye-catching creations. But, as with all forms of dress, outrageous hat fashions are not a new phenomenon.

Causing a sensation

Very often a hat style gradually becomes more extreme. That is how, in the 1800s, neat and simple bonnets grew into outsize fashion statements. Hat-makers often stick to the style and shape that is fashionable at the moment, but exaggerate it to make the hat stand out.

Costume hat

This French postcard of the 1920s shows a cloche hat – it is decorated with a huge spider's web!

Silly seaside hats

Every era has its fashion victims. In the 1800s, men fell for top hats that stretched ever taller – while their wives wanted bonnets that spread out ever wider.

Taken to extremes

The poke-bonnet's brim shaded the wearer – but could be absurdly large.

Dazzling designers

The best milliners do more than rehash old ideas. They create wearable works of art that express the feelings of the time. One of the most imaginative was Elsa Schiaparelli (1890–1973). Her creations were inspired by Surrealism, an art movement that found beauty in the absurd.

Key designers since then include Simone Mirman (*b.*1920), whose crazy, floppy hats captured the mood of the 1960s. In the 1980s, Graham Smith (*b.*1938) made big, bold hats for power-dressing women. And, since setting up in 1990, Philip Treacy (*b.*1967) has built a reputation for hats in amazing shapes!

Sassy Schiaparelli

Schiaparelli's designs included hats shaped like shoes or lamb chops! She collaborated on these with Surrealist artist Salvador Dalí (1904–89).

Ladies' Day at Royal Ascot

The cream of designer hats are worn to the Ascot races. Some of the wackiest hats are worn by Mrs Shilling, mother of milliner David Shilling (b.1953). He designed his first Ascot hat at the age of 12!

Treacy hat

Irish milliner Philip Treacy is known for his outsize, sculptural designs. Many of his hats seem to twist up towards the sky. Treacy opened his own London hat shop in 1990.

Hat & hair technology

ALTHOUGH MANY HATS ARE NOW MADE IN FACTORIES, *hat-making techniques have changed little over the centuries. Factory machines mimic the methods used by milliners.*

How to...

The traditional way to make a felt or straw hat by hand is to use a hatter's block. This is made of wood or, more usually nowadays, aluminium. Felt and straw are the most commonly used hat materials. Both need to be mulled, or dampened with steam, so they will be easy to mould into shape on the hatter's block. The crown is shaped first, then the brim is added. Next, the hat is stiffened with a special gum-like solution, so that it will not lose its shape. Finally, the hat is trimmed with a band or ribbons.

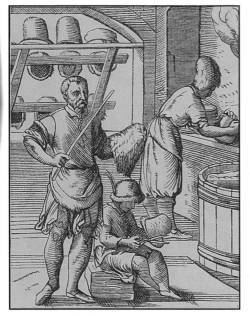

Mad as a hatter

In the past, hatters used mercury salts for felt-making, unaware it was poisonous. As a result, many hatters became ill with a mental disorder called erethism.

Top trims

Hats for special occasions are artistically trimmed with net veils, fake flowers and huge bows of satin ribbon.

Advert

Wavy hair was fashionable in the 1920s and 1930s. To achieve the look, women could buy all sorts of gadgets.

SET YOUR O

YOU CAN SET YOUR WAVE
The BUTYWAVE WAVESETTER, designed
modern hairdressers, will set your waves, a
entirely automatic—there are no "messy
little or weak.

ADJUSTED IN A SECOND
the BUTYWAVE WAVESETTER can be
hairdressing in a few seconds. Glance a
simple it is. The pictures are actual photo
pressed gently into deep, natural waves, whi
wearing the BUTYWAVE WAVESETTER

O COMFORTABLE YOU
the BUTYWAVE WAVESETTER has
ou've got it on, it's so comfortable.
complete comfort.

YOU SAVE MONEY TOO
think! 5/- is all you have to pay for
nience of periodical visits to the ha

5/- BUT
WA

btainable from all high-class Drapers
case of difficulty post coupon to

To The Butywave Co., 10
Dear Sir,—Please send it
WAVING CAPS, for which

NAME

Hair-raising wigs & transplants

Long ago, wigs were the only option for someone wishing to disguise baldness. Wigs can be made of real or synthetic hair. Most are mass-produced, but some are handmade for a perfect fit. The wig-maker makes a net cap to fit the client's head, then tucks in tufts of hair with a hook-shaped needle. Each tuft is securely knotted by hand, and making a wig can take around 40,000 knots.

These days, some people choose a permanent, surgical remedy instead, with hair transplants.

PLUG-IN HAIR

The transplant surgeon fills the bald area with plugs (sections of scalp containing about 10 hairs). The process is extremely fiddly. It takes several sessions to transplant enough plugs to cover the average bald patch.

WIG WORKERS IN NEW YORK

This is what a wig production line looked like 80 years ago. Employees fashioned piles of human hair into wigs by hand.

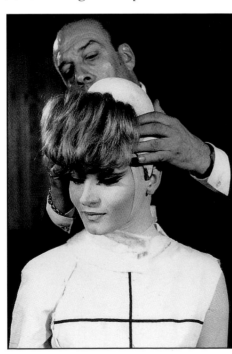

FINAL FIT

Hairpieces, like this one from the sixties, are expensive if made-to-measure. 'Off-the-peg' models are cheaper.

Hats off to hair care

Hair fashions change, as new inventions appear. In 1904, a German hairdresser demonstrated the permanent wave or perm and soon curly styles became easier for everyone to achieve. Electric dryers, clippers, crimpers, curlers and straighteners have all revolutionized how people style their hair. Sprays, gels, mousses, waxes and other products also influence fashionable styles – and will continue to do so.

Timeline

Prehistory

Early peoples may have cut their hair for special rites – or hacked it off when it got in the way of hunting. Fur hoods were worn for warmth.

The ancient world

The ancient Egyptians wore glossy wigs over shaved heads. Pharaohs wore crowns. Greek and Roman women braided, curled and dyed their hair. Soldiers wore protective helmets of leather or bronze.

The Middle Ages

In the 1100s, women covered their hair with a coverchief, shawl or mantle. Royals and nobles wore crowns and coronets. Fantastically tall horned headdresses and steeple-hats were fashionable from the 1200s. Men's hair was cut short with a thick, round fringe. The fashionable man wore a bourrelet on his head, this was covered with a hood called a chaperon.

16th century

Men began to wear a stiff, felt cap. Around 1530 the soft, halo-brimmed bonnet made an appearance. Towards the end of the century, noblewomen began to curl their hair and adorn it with jewels. Elizabeth I of England (1533–1603) set a trend for red hair and wigs.

17th century

Fashionable men at the turn of the century wore the tall-crowned capotain hat. This later became the Puritan's sugarloaf hat, which was worn over short hair. Puritan women wore simple caps. The nobility wore low-crowned, wide-brimmed hats over long, wavy hair. Ladies wore their hair in ringlets and a braided knot at the back.

18th century

For most of the 1700s, women frizzed and curled their hair with curling irons to create big styles that were often covered with pomade (styling grease) and white powder. The fashionable man wore a wig, topped with a three-cornered tricorn hat or, later, the two-cornered bicorn. In the late 1700s, wigs were abandoned for a more natural look. Bandeaux, turbans and ostrich feathers were popular evening headwear for women.

19th century

By 1840 women usually wore their hair in a bun, with ringlets framing the face. The poke-bonnet was worn with wide-skirted dresses. Fashionable men wore top hats, while workers wore flat-caps. At the end of the century, women's hairstyles grew taller. Large hats became fashionable, too.

20th century & beyond

The permanent wave was invented by Karl Nessler in 1904, paving the way for wavy, short styles in the 1920s. The Eton crop became fashionable. Close-fitting cloche hats were worn by day; bandeaux in the evening. For men, the short-back-and-sides hairstyle became fashionable. In the 1930s, marcelling was popular – styling women's hair with the curling tongs invented by Marcel Grateau in the 1870s. In World War II (1939–45), women adopted headscarves to protect the hair from dirt and machinery. In the 1950s the full, bouffant hairstyle became popular with women, but required weekly setting at the salon. It developed into the tall, beehive styles of the early 1960s. Then, Vidal Sassoon invented his low-maintenance bob that only required cutting every six weeks and was widely copied. In the 1970s, hippy fashions arrived – men and women wore their hair long. Street styles, such as punk mohicans, were fashionable with the young. The designer hat became popular for special occasions. Since the 1990s, young men – and some women – have favoured short, cropped styles. Spray-on dyes and hair extensions have also offered more flexibility for people wanting to change their look in an instant.

Glossary

Bandeau

A strip of decorative cloth that is wrapped around the head, usually for evening wear.

Bouffant

Describes the full, puffed-out hairstyles popular during the 1950s.

Brim

The projecting edging around a hat.

Cap

A hat without a brim, or with a very small brim or visor at the front.

Chignon

A soft bun or coil of hair worn at the back of the neck.

Coif

A close-fitting cap, or the band at the front of a nun's headdress.

Crown

The rounded part of a hat and a hat, usually a metal circlet, worn by monarchs.

Felt

A compacted cloth, made from wool, fur or hair, compressed in hot, damp conditions.

Fillet

A medieval band that tied around the head, often decorated with jewels. The term may also describe a hairnet to hold long hair.

Five-point bob

A short style invented by Vidal Sassoon in 1964. The hair was cut into points either side of the ears and at the nape of the neck.

Hennin

A type of steeple-hat – a tall, conical hat with a floaty veil, worn by medieval ladies.

Milliner

A hat-maker or hatter.

Millinery

Hats, or the materials needed to make hats.

Plush

Extremely soft silk or, sometimes, cotton, where the surface has been brushed so that small fibres stand up, as they do on velvet.

Tip

The top part of a hat's crown.

Tweed

A coarse, wool cloth woven into a pattern, popular for coats and suits.

Wimple

A lady's veil that is folded to frame the face. It is still sometimes part of a nun's dress.

Index